Poison Pen Mystery

Janet Lorimer

LEARNING · DEVELOPMENT · AIDS
LDA

The Poison Pen Mystery
LD875Z
ISBN 1 85503 011 X

Published under licence in the UK by LDA

First published in UK 1990

LDA, Duke Street, Wisbech, Cambs., PE13 2AE England

Printed in Great Britain by Ebenezer Baylis and Son Ltd,
The Trinity Press, Worcester, and London.

CHAPTER

1

Waiting for the Guests

"Something is going to go wrong this weekend," Susan Miller said suddenly. "I just know it!"

Her husband, Paul, threw down the magazine he'd been reading. "Cut it out, Susan," he groaned. "You'll make yourself sick if you don't stop worrying. Nothing is going to go wrong. We've thought of everything to make this weekend a success. Everyone is going to have a wonderful time."

Susan sighed. "I hope you're right," she said.

There was a loud roll of thunder overhead. Paul went to the window and pulled the curtains open. He grinned at his wife. "Even the weather is on our side," he said. "There's a big storm rolling in. Just think how great it will be when we all gather in the library after dinner.

The candles will make the room dim. Thunder will roll, lightning will flash!" He dropped his voice to a whisper. "Best of all, there will be a feeling of danger and evil lurking about!"

Susan shivered, but she couldn't help smiling. "You're beginning to scare me," she said. "Speaking of candles, what if that storm knocks the power out? Do we have enough candles?"

Paul sighed. "Several boxes of them," he said in a normal voice. "Come on, honey, will you please stop worrying? I tell you, we've thought of everything." He looked his wife up and down. "Susan, that dress looks great on you. You should have lived 100 years ago. I love those long dresses that sweep the floor."

"You wouldn't love this dress so much if you had to wear it," she said. "Every time I take a step, I trip over the hem. I'll be glad to put on modern clothes tomorrow. And how do you like that stiff collar you're wearing?"

Paul tugged at the collar. "You're right," he said. "These Victorian clothes look great, but it isn't much fun to wear them. On the other hand, our guests are going to enjoy seeing us in them. Yes, this is going to be the best weekend the Masters of Mystery have ever had."

He sat down and picked up his magazine. For a moment Susan watched him. Paul was a tall, thin man. Tonight he was dressed in a Victorian suit with a long coat, and his shirt had that high stiff collar. He looked good, Susan thought, even if his short hair and modern glasses seemed out of place.

Susan glanced around the room. Paul was right. They had thought of everything. These Victorian clothes. This wonderful old Victorian house they had rented for the weekend. She had to smile when she thought of the rooms filled with heavy furniture. Even the bathtubs upstairs had the old-fashioned claw feet. It was all perfect for putting their guests in the right mood.

Paul and Susan Miller owned a small bookshop in New York. The shop was a "specialty" bookshop — the Millers sold only books of mystery and suspense. Mystery stories were the great interest in their lives. Many of their friends had the same interest. Because they were usually so busy, they didn't get to see each other very often.

Then, a few years before, they had come up with a great idea. Each year they would set one weekend aside and spend it together. During that weekend they would talk about their favourite subject. They would take turns playing host for these weekends. They even gave their group a name — the Masters of Mystery.

Last year the hosts had added something special to the weekend. A theme. And for that weekend, the theme had been famous detectives. The members had not only talked about famous detectives, they had also played guessing games and solved puzzles with the same theme.

This year it was the Millers' turn to host the weekend. After they had picked their theme, they decided to go one step further. They rented a large Victorian house out in the country. It was almost 15 miles from the nearest town. A narrow dirt road led to the house through the dark woods.

In addition, Paul and Susan had decided to wear Victorian clothes on Friday night. Susan had planned meals that were popular 100 years ago. No one but Paul and Susan knew what the theme was. But the house, their clothes, and the food would give a few clues. Their friends would have fun guessing the theme until Paul and Susan told them after dinner.

Suddenly Susan was pulled from her thoughts by the sound of raindrops hitting the window. "Paul," she said, "It's started to rain. What if our guests get lost in this storm? This old house is so far out of the way."

"There you go again," Paul sighed. "Look, I sent everyone a good map. Now, why don't you sit down and take a look at this magazine. There's a short story in it by Teri Callahan. One of the first short stories she ever wrote. It's been reprinted in this issue. Why don't you read it? It will take your mind off the weekend."

"I'm sorry, Paul," Susan said. "But I can't forget what happened at our weekend last year. I don't want it to be like that again this year."

"What are you talking about?" her husband asked.

"Remember what an awful mood Basil was in? And Teri, too."

"Hold on," Paul said. "You're looking on the dark side, Susan. Basil was only worried about finding one more short story for that book of mystery stories he wanted to publish. By the end of the weekend, he was feeling much better. And he got the story he needed a couple of weeks after that. So it all worked out."

"And Teri —"

"Teri was a little nervous because she was trying to finish her latest book. She was also fine by the end of the weekend. In fact, she was in such a good mood that she wanted to cook dinner."

Susan made a face. "And burned the steaks! Teri is a terrible cook."

Paul laughed. "We all kidded her about the cooking. But she was a good sport. She went out and bought more steaks."

"And let someone else cook them," Susan added. "That was a good thing. Or we might not have had anything to eat that night."

"The point is that the weekend turned out okay," Paul said. "Friday night is always hard because it's the end of a busy week and everyone is tired."

"Oh, you're right," Susan said. "I am worrying about nothing and —"

"Listen," Paul said. "I think I hear a car driving up."

CHAPTER

2

Basil's Surprise

The person Paul heard driving up was their first guest, Basil Hunter. When they opened the front door, Basil hurried in out of the rain. He put his suitcase down and gave Susan a big hug. "What a night!" he said, taking off his coat.

"Come into the library where it's warm," Susan said. "Would you like some coffee?"

"Sounds great," Basil said. Then he added, "Where are the others?"

"You're the first," Paul said, putting more wood on the fire.

"I'm the first guest or —" He stopped.

Paul looked puzzled. "Or what?"

"Oh, nothing," Basil said, smiling to himself. "Well I'm sure the others will be along soon." He held his hands out to warm them over the fire. "It's good to see you two. Susan, you look beautiful, like a woman who just stepped out of the pages of a Victorian novel. Am I right in thinking that these clothes you and Paul are wearing have something to do with the theme of this weekend?"

Susan smiled as she handed him a cup of coffee. "That's right," she said. "And you can guess all you want. We aren't telling until after dinner."

Basil laughed. He was a tall man with iron grey hair and a small moustache. Basil was a book publisher. Most of the books he published were mysteries. Paul and Susan sold a lot of his books in their bookshop. Basil's books always sold well.

While the three were talking, there was a loud banging on the front door. "I guess another member of the Masters of Mystery is here," Susan said.

It was Stephanie Wells, Basil's niece. She was a young woman in her early twenties with long blonde hair and soft blue eyes. She worked as a secretary for her uncle.

"What awful weather!" Stephanie said as she hurried into the house. "I hope it won't ruin the weekend."

"Paul says it will add to the mood," Susan

said. She hung up Stephanie's coat and showed her into the library. Susan was pouring coffee for Stephanie when there was another knock at the front door.

"I'll get it," Paul said. A few moments later he brought Jerry and Mona Rice into the library. Jerry was a short, plump man with thinning hair. Five years before he had retired from the Police Force. After he had retired, he had opened his own detective agency.

His wife, Mona, was an editor. She worked for Basil Hunter, too. Mona was a small, thin woman with greying hair. Susan noticed that tonight Mona looked a little pale. "Are you feeling all right?" Susan asked as she handed Mona a cup of coffee.

Mona gave Susan a weak smile. "Just tired," she said. "It's been a long week."

"Well, we're all here," Paul said. "Except for Teri, of course. I hope she doesn't get lost."

"Or get her car stuck in the mud," Jerry said. "That dirt road out there was supposed to be used by a horse and carriage, not a car."

"I wouldn't worry about Teri," Basil said.

"She's driving a new car, you know."

"*Another* new car?" Susan said. "What does she do, buy a new one every year?"

"I wish I could do that," Stephanie sighed. "It must be great to be so rich."

Basil laughed. "All you have to do is write a new book every year," he said. "That's how Teri does it."

"I think I hear another car," Susan said. She hurried to open the front door. Teri came running in out of the rain. She was a tall redhead. She was wearing a long fur coat, and high black leather boots. Diamonds sparkled on her ears and fingers.

"Am I late?" she said, handing Susan the fur coat. "I had the worst time getting here."

"You're right on time," Susan said, rubbing the coat against her cheek. "What a beautiful coat, Teri."

"What a beautiful price tag," Teri laughed. "But it was worth it. Speaking of clothes, I love that dress you're wearing. Were we supposed to wear Victorian clothes this weekend?"

"No," Susan said. "Paul and I did it because we thought it would help set the mood for our theme."

"What is the theme?" Teri asked as they walked into the library.

"It's a surprise," Paul said. "Well, we're all here. The Masters of Mystery meet again! And now —"

Suddenly there was more loud banging on the front door. Paul and Susan looked surprised. "Who could that be?" Susan asked.

Basil laughed. "Surprise, surprise," he said. "Let's go and find out."

He hurried to the front door with the others trailing behind. When he opened the door, they saw two very wet, cold people standing outside. Basil told them to come right in.

"Paul, Susan, I have a little surprise for you. I don't know the theme for the weekend. But when you told me you had rented this Victorian house, I decided you would need some help with the cooking and cleaning. Meet your butler and maid. Bert Jarvis and Lynn Cutler."

For a moment, Paul and Susan didn't know what to say. Then Susan said, "Well, this is a surprise! Come in and take off those wet coats." She tried to sound pleased.

"Yes," Paul said. "Welcome to a weekend with the Masters of Mystery."

Bert laughed. "Masters of what?"

Lynn poked him sharply. "Be nice, Bert! Hi, Mr. Hunter. Sorry we're late. But we had a little trouble finding the place. We'll get into our working clothes right away. If you could just show us to our rooms, we —."

"Rooms!" Susan turned to Paul. "Oh, my goodness! Where are we going to put them?"

"Don't worry, we'll find something," Paul said. Then to Bert and Lynn he added, "We cleaned only the rooms we planned to use this weekend. As you can see, this is a big place. There are three floors of rooms, as well as an attic and a cellar. But I think there are two empty bedrooms on the second floor you can use."

"I bet we have to clean them up first," Bert said crossly.

"Stop it, Bert!" Lynn said. Then to Susan, she added, "Don't mind Bert. He's in a bad mood because we had to drive so far. But he'll snap out of it. And he's really a good worker. Come on, Bert, you're supposed to be a butler. Act like one!"

Bert picked up his suitcase and followed Paul up the stairs. Lynn trailed behind with her suitcase. As soon as they were gone, Susan led the others back to the library.

"All right, Basil," she said. "What's this all about? Who are those people?"

Basil looked very unhappy. "They aren't what I thought they would be. You see, I went through an agency that sends out maids and butlers to help with parties. I talked to Lynn, but this is the first time I've met Bert. I just wanted you and Paul to have as much fun as we will this weekend. I expected serious people. This was going to be my gift to you. I'm afraid it isn't turning out the way I hoped it would."

Susan smiled. "Well, it was a nice thought," she said. "And I thank you for thinking about us."

"But I hadn't counted on that young man with his smart mouth," Basil said. "Some butler he turned out to be!"

"Once they get settled into their rooms, I'm sure they'll be fine," Susan said. Then, seeing the look on Stephanie's face, Susan added, "What's wrong, Steph?"

"I know that woman from somewhere," Stephanie said. "But I can't remember where."

"Susan, would you mind showing us to our rooms?" Mona said suddenly. "I'm really tired. I'd like to rest for a while before dinner."

"Of course not," Susan said quickly. "Are you sure you feel all right?"

"I'm just tired," Mona said. "I've been working very hard, and you know what Fridays are like."

Susan nodded. "Come on, everyone. I'll show you where the bedrooms are. I hope you like your rooms. The beds are quite comfortable, and there is a fireplace in each room."

"Are we using candles?" Basil asked. "Or is there something modern to light our way, like torches?"

Susan laughed. "Electric lights," she said.

"I don't mind candles," Stephanie said. "As long as I can have a hot bath before bed."

"There's plenty of hot water," Susan told her. "But I have to tell you that there are only two bathrooms. So Paul and I have set one aside for the women, and the other one is for the men. Wait till you see the bathtubs with their claw feet! They've been here since the house was built 100 years ago!"

After Susan showed her guests to their rooms, she went back to the kitchen. Thanks to Basil, she now had two more people to feed. She hoped she had enough food on hand. She told herself that Basil had only wanted to help her by hiring a butler and maid. But she wished he had picked another gift, one that didn't eat! Then she told herself that she was not being very kind. Bert and Lynn would probably turn out to be a big help.

Paul came into the kitchen while Susan was washing the potatoes.

"Did you get Bert and Lynn settled into their rooms?" Susan asked.

Paul made a face. "Yes, but not without a lot of wisecracks from Bert. Lynn seems like she could be a big help, though."

"Did you find out anything more about them?" Susan said.

"They're both college students," Paul said. "They take on these kinds of jobs to earn a little extra money."

"What are they studying?" Susan asked.

"English literature," Paul said. "Lynn wants to be a writer. I think she plans to write a masterpiece. Bert has other plans. I think he wants to teach in college. There is one thing you should know about Bert. He thinks mystery stories are rubbish!"

Susan rolled her eyes. "Oh, wonderful! That's all we need this weekend."

"I told him to keep his opinions to himself," Paul said. "He's just here to do a job. How about everyone else? Did they get settled in okay?"

Susan nodded. "And they're all trying to guess the theme for the weekend. By the way, did you put the clues for our game in the library?"

Paul nodded. "An axe, one knife, and one teacup with saucer." Then, Paul grinned and rubbed his hands together. "Three clues to our theme of 'unsolved crimes' " He began to sing, "Lizzie Borden took an axe, and gave her mother 40 whacks. When she saw what she had done —"

"Paul!"

" — she gave her father 41. What's wrong?"

"Someone may hear you," Susan said. "You'll give the whole thing away."

"Don't be silly," Paul laughed. "No one can hear us. Besides, everyone's upstairs."

"I wonder where our maid and butler are," Susan said, filling a pan with water. "We still have a lot to do. I have to set the table and —" She stopped and listened. "What was that?"

"What was what?"

"That sound. It came from the dining room." Susan hurried to open the door between the dining room and kitchen. She looked into the dining room.

"Well?" Paul asked. "Is Jack the Ripper hiding under the table?"

"I was sure I heard someone," Susan said. "But there's no one there now."

"It's just your imagination," Paul said. "Old houses make strange noises."

Susan shut the door again. She didn't say anything more. But she still had a funny feeling that someone had been in the dining room — and listening.

CHAPTER

3

An Unknown Author

Susan was putting the final touches on dinner when Bert and Lynn appeared. Bert had changed into a dark suit. Lynn was wearing a black dress with a white apron. They looked like a butler and maid.

"Let me do that, Mrs. Miller," Lynn said. "You don't want to spill anything on that pretty dress."

Susan told Lynn what the plans were for dinner. Then she went to meet their guests in the dining room. As the guests were being seated, Susan said, "Where's Stephanie?"

"She was in the bathroom putting on fresh make-up," Mona said.

As Bert was bringing in the first course, Stephanie appeared. "Sorry I'm late," she said. "Paul does this house have a secret passage?"

"Not that I know of," Paul said. "Why?"

"Well, the wall by the bathtub sounds hollow."

Jerry laughed. "So that's what you were doing! Tapping the walls."

Stephanie turned red. "I thought I could figure out what the theme was before Paul and Susan told us," she said.

Suddenly Jerry snapped his fingers. "I've got it! We're going to play a real live game of Cluedo this weekend. I think it was Mr. Green with the knife in the ballroom. Is there a ballroom in this house?"

Paul laughed. "No, Jerry. You're way off course."

"Oh, come on," Mona said. "Tell us what the theme is, Paul!"

"After dinner," Susan said. "Come on, everyone. Don't let the food get cold."

At that moment there was a loud roll of thunder and the lights went dim. Everyone was startled. Teri gave a cry. She had spilled her soup in her lap. She pushed her chair back from the table. "Oh, now look what I've done," she said.

Lynn grabbed a cloth and began to wipe it up. Teri pushed Lynn's hand away. "Don't! You'll only make it worse," she said. "I'd better go upstairs and change." She hurried from the room.

"Tell me, Paul, did you specially order this storm to go along with the weekend?" Basil asked. "It's perfect!"

"Gothics!" Stephanie said. "That's it, isn't it! The weekend theme has something to do with gothic mysteries. You know, the stories with the strange old house in the middle of nowhere. All the characters behave oddly, violence and danger are always lurking behind a locked door or in a dusty attic and —"

"And a young woman always runs around screaming in her nightgown," Mona said, laughing. "Well, if that is the theme, you can count me out. I wouldn't be caught dead running around outdoors in weather like this. And not in a thin nightgown!"

Susan smiled. "Don't worry, Mona, you're safe. The theme isn't gothic mysteries. But it would have been a good one, wouldn't it? It's a shame those books aren't as popular as they used to be."

"Speaking of books," Paul said, "Your newest book is doing very well, Basil. Susan and I have sold a lot of copies, of it."

"You bet," Basil grinned. "We're printing

50,000 more copies next month. *Mysteries for Midnight Reading* is the most popular short-story collection we've ever published."

"Isn't that the one you were so worried about a year ago?" Jerry said.

Basil nodded. "That's right. But everything worked out after all. If you remember, the last time we met, I was worried about finding one more story for the book."

"What happened?" Susan said.

"Well, a couple of weeks after our weekend, I got the perfect story in the mail. It's one of the best mysteries I've ever read!"

"That's the story by J. R. Thompson, isn't it?" Paul asked. "I agree, Basil. It's the best story in the book."

Teri came back to the dining room. "What's the best story?" she said.

"The one in Basil's new book," Susan said. "We were just talking about how popular the book is."

"Well, who is J. R. Thompson, anyway?" Paul asked.

Basil shook his head. "You've got me," he said. "I don't even know if the writer is a man or a woman. It's quite a mystery."

"You mean you haven't met the writer?" Susan said.

"No," Basil said. "The return address was a post office box. After I read the story, I wrote to the writer and asked if we could meet. I'd like to publish more stories by J. R. Thompson."

"And?" Susan said.

"And nothing. J. R. Thompson wrote back to say that it was out of the question. The writer did not want to meet with me or send me any more stories or promote the book in any way."

"That's crazy," Paul said. "Teri, why wouldn't the writer want that publicity?"

Teri shrugged. "It's hard to say. Sometimes the price of being rich and famous is too high!"

"What do you mean?" Susan asked.

"Well, look at me," Teri said. "I never get to take a break. If I don't write a new book every year, my 'fans' get upset."

"So you have to keep working. But you do it," Susan said. "By the way, when are you coming out with a new book? Weren't you working on one last year?

"I'm still working on it," Teri said. "It's going to be a long book, and I've had to make a lot of changes. That takes time."

"Maybe you should be writing short

stories," Susan said. "They don't take much time to write, I bet. Well, not as much time as a novel."

"I don't like to write short stories," Teri said. "I like working with a long novel. It gives me room to develop my plot and my characters." Then she turned to Basil. "So J. R. Thompson is a bit of a mystery."

"That's right," Basil said. "I did everything I could to find out who that writer is. I even hired Jerry to check into it."

They all looked at Jerry but he, too, shrugged. "I tried everything I could think of to find the writer," he said. "But I had no luck. There is no J. R. Thompson living in that area. I guess the writer made the name up to keep Basil from finding out who he or she really is. I even watched the post office for a while, hoping this writer would show up to get the mail. Unfortunately, no one ever did."

Lynn and Bert began to remove the plates. Basil pushed his chair back with a groan of pleasure. "What a meal!" he said. "Susan, you're a wonderful cook."

"Why, thank you," she said. "I hope you saved enough room for my famous almond pudding."

Jerry groaned. "Have you forgotten that some of us are watching our weight?"

Susan laughed. "I won't make you eat any, Jerry, not if you really don't want to."

"You're a cruel woman, Susan Miller," Jerry said. "How can I pass up your almond pudding?"

"Almonds!" Stephanie said. "Isn't there a poison that smells like almonds?"

"What are you saying?" Paul asked with a laugh. "Do you think Susan is planning to poison you all?"

"Oh, no," Stephanie said. "I just thought maybe that was the theme for the weekend. Poisons."

"I hope not," Mona said darkly. "I'd like to be able to enjoy my meals."

"Don't worry," Susan said. "I'm not going to poison anyone. Lynn, would you please bring in the pudding."

CHAPTER

4

Clues to a Theme

At the end of the meal, Susan asked everyone to go into the library. "I'll have Lynn bring us some coffee," she said.

"I'm going to run upstairs and get a sweater," Stephanie said. "I'm getting cold."

"I'll go with you," Mona said. "I want to get my knitting. It always helps me think."

As soon as Mona and Stephanie returned, Paul said, "And now the game begins. I'll show you some clues to the theme. The first person who guesses it wins a prize."

"Oh, good," Stephanie said. "What's the prize, Paul? Dinner with Sherlock Holmes?"

"It beats a date with Jack the Ripper," Teri said, grinning.

Paul put a large box on the table, pulled out an axe, and held it up.

Stephanie shivered. "That's a scary looking thing."

"What! No blood on the blade?" Basil laughed.

"And no fingerprints on the handle," Susan said. "Okay, anyone want to guess?"

"Killers we've known and loved?" said Teri.

Paul shook his head. There was a moment of silence while everyone thought. Paul reached into the box for the second clue. He pulled out a teacup and saucer.

"I knew it!" Stephanie said. "Poison!"

"Wrong again," Susan laughed.

"And now," Paul said, "Last but not —" He frowned and looked into the box. "That's strange. It's not here."

"I thought you checked everything," Susan said.

"I did," Paul said. "It was here before dinner. I can't figure out . . . . Oh, well, don't worry. I'll get another one." He hurried from the room.

The guests stared at the axe and the teacup. "Both of these things could be used as weapons," Terry said. "Is that it? Weapons?"

"Sorry," Susan said. "Anyone else care to guess?"

"I think the theme has something to do with this old house and those clothes you're wearing. They have to fit in with the other clues," Mona said.

"Right," Jerry said. "When good old Queen Victoria ruled half the world. There were plenty of good mysteries in those days."

"Like Sherlock Holmes," Stephanie said. "Detectives of 100 years ago."

At that moment Paul returned. He had his hands behind his back. "And now for the last clue," he said. He held up a small knife.

"Paul." Susan said. "Where's the big knife?"

"I don't know," he said. "I thought it was in the box. I can't find it in the kitchen, and Lynn says she didn't use it to cut the meat."

Susan groaned. "That's my best knife!"

"A knife, an axe, and a teacup," Basil said slowly. He and the others looked puzzled. "Wait a minute," Basil said. "Does the theme have anything to do with Lizzie Borden? Famous women killers?"

"That would explain the axe and the teacup," Teri said. "But not the knife."

"Jack the Ripper," Mona said suddenly.

"You're getting warm," Paul said.

"But what does a teacup have to do with Jack the Ripper?" Jerry asked.

"Madeleine Smith!" Teri said, snapping her fingers.

"Who's that?" Stepanie asked.

"Madeleine Smith was supposed to have killed her boyfriend with poison," Teri said. "But the jury let her go. They couldn't prove it."

"And Florence Bravo," Jerry said. "Same story. She was supposed to have killed her husband with poison, but they couldn't prove it."

"Would Dr. Crippin fit the theme?" Teri asked. "He killed his wife."

Paul shook his head. "No, but Constance Kent would."

"Wait a minute," Basil said excitedly. "Constance Kent was set free, too. I think we're on to something here. Lizzie Borden was set free even though many people believed she killed her father and her stepmother with an axe.

"No one ever figured out who Jack the Ripper was," Stephanie said. "All of these cases happened around 100 years ago, during the reign of Queen Victoria. That's it!" She sat up straight, looking excited. "Unsolved crimes of the Victorian age."

"You got it!" Susan cried.

"What's my prize?" Stephanie asked.

"You get the first hot bath," Susan laughed.

"Thanks a lot!" Stephanie said. "Some prize!"

"We'll make sure no one murders you in your bath," Basil said cheerfully.

Stephanie shivered. "Thanks, Uncle Basil! Now I *will* have bad dreams tonight."

Basil laughed. "Speaking of dreams," he said, "I'm ready to turn in. It's been a long day."

"Me, too," Mona said. "I'm ready to call it a night. How about you, Jerry?"

Her husband nodded. "You'd better get started on that bath, Stephanie. My wife will be right behind you."

"And don't use up all the hot water," Teri added.

"Okay," Stephanie said, heading off.

"I guess I'd better go and see how Bert and Lynn are doing," Susan said. Then, as she saw Mona heading for the door, she added, "Don't forget your knitting, Mona."

Mona looked at Susan in surprise. "I'd

forget my head if it wasn't attached to my neck," she laughed. "I'm so tired I'm not thinking straight."

"What are you knitting?" Susan asked.

"A pair of socks for Jerry," Mona said. "Except one is a size too big and the other one is a size too small. I guess knitting is not my thing. I'm just a beginner, you see."

The two women said good-night at the bottom of the stairs, and Susan went into the kitchen. To her surprise, all the food had been put away and the dishes had been washed and stacked in the cupboards. The coffee pot and cups and saucers were on the kitchen table. Everything was ready for breakfast.

"Not bad," Susan said to herself. "It looks like I was wrong about the maid and butler. They may be a big help after all. As she was leaving the kitchen, she heard a loud scream. It came from the second floor.

CHAPTER

5

Two Mysterious Notes

Susan raced up the stairs. She found the others in the hall crowded around Stephanie. The young woman was leaning against the wall, her hands over her face, crying.

Basil put his arm around his niece's shoulder. "What is it, Stephanie? What's the matter?"

Stephanie pointed at the bathroom. The others crowded into the doorway to see what had upset her so much.

On the wall over the bathtub was a note. It was pinned to the wall with a large knife. Drops of red dripped from the blade and trickled down the wall.

Susan felt her stomach turn. She put her hand over her mouth and closed her eyes. Paul pushed past his wife into the bathroom. He pulled the knife and the note from the wall, and read the note aloud.

"Jack was clever with his knife.
He stole the precious gift of life.
Another thief is here today,
But unlike Jack, this thief will pay!"

Susan opened her eyes. "What in the world does it mean?" she asked.

"That's a good question," Paul said. He sniffed the blade. "This isn't blood, it's sauce."

"Sauce?" Stephanie cried. "I thought —"

"— that it was blood?" Paul finished. "That's what you were supposed to think, I guess."

"Is this your idea of a joke?" Teri snapped at Paul.

"Hold on," Susan said. "Paul and I didn't do this."

"Then who did?" Teri asked.

"How do we know this isn't supposed to be another little surprise for the weekend?" Basil said. He looked very angry.

"I tell you, Susan and I had nothing to do with this," Paul said.

"Is that the missing knife?" Jerry asked.

Susan nodded. "But how did it get up here?"

"Someone must have taken it out of the box before dinner," Paul said.

"What does that poem mean?" Mona asked. "We were talking about Jack the Ripper in the library. But I don't remember anything about a thief."

The others shook their heads. They all looked puzzled.

"It doesn't make sense," Jerry said. "Unless it's someone's sick idea of a joke."

"Well, it's not funny," Stephanie said. "And if this is how the weekend is going to go, I don't want to stay! I'm going to get my suitcase and —"

"Now hold on," Basil said. "Don't be silly, Stephanie. After all, it's nearly midnight. It's dark and it's raining. That road is going to be a sea of mud. It's just too dangerous for you to leave now."

"I don't care!" Stephanie snapped. "What am I supposed to do, stay here and get my throat cut?"

"Take it easy," Teri said. "No one's going to cut your throat. You're just a little scared, that's all. Look, why don't you spend the night in my room? I have twin beds and we can lock the door from the inside. That should make you feel safe."

"Oh, really? And just why should I trust you, Teri? Maybe *you* wrote that note!"

"Me?" Teri cried. "Now why would I do that?"

"Hold on," Jerry said loudly. "Why would any of us leave that note? We're all friends, remember? Nothing like this has ever happened before."

"That's right," Paul said. "It's just us."

"Oh, no," Susan said. "Bert and Lynn. You don't think they —"

"It's possible," Jerry said. "We don't really know anything about them, do we?"

"That's right," Paul said. "Besides, Bert told me that he thinks mystery stories are rubbish."

"Stephanie, you thought you knew Lynn from somewhere," Susan said. "Can't you remember?"

Stephanie shook her head. "But I'll keep trying," she said. Then she turned to Teri. "I'm sorry I got mad at you. I was scared, but I shouldn't have taken it out on you."

"That's okay," Teri said. "Now I think we should all turn in. What are you going to do about Bert and Lynn, Paul?"

"I'll have a talk with them in the morning," Paul said. "If one of them is behind this note, I'll probably send them packing. We don't want anything to ruin the weekend."

"I wish I hadn't hired them," Basil said. "I guess it was a stupid idea."

"You couldn't know that this would happen," Susan said. She went into the bathroom to clean up the mess. Mona stayed to help. "You know," Mona said. "It's funny that Bert and Lynn aren't around."

"What do you mean?" Susan said.

"Their rooms are just down the hall. They must have heard Stephanie scream. I wonder why they didn't come to see what was wrong."

"Maybe one of them *is* guilty," Susan said. "Or maybe they just think screams in the night are part of our weekend fun. I keep thinking about the note. Why do you suppose the poem mentioned a thief?"

Mona shrugged. "Maybe Paul will get some answers in the morning."

"I hope so," Susan said. "This was not part of the plan, Mona. I just hope the rest of the weekend goes well."

Even though Susan couldn't stop thinking about the strange note, she didn't have any trouble falling asleep. It had been a long hard day for her, too. But it seemed that no sooner had she fallen asleep than there was a soft tapping on the door. Susan woke up to find grey light streaming through the window. It was morning already!

"Paul," she whispered. "Someone's at the door."

"I know, I know," he said. He put his foot on the floor and pulled it back quickly. "It's cold in here," he said with a shiver.

"You answer the door, and I'll start a fire in the fireplace," Susan said.

Paul hurried across the icy floor and opened the door. Lynn was standing in the hall. She looked frightened.

"What's wrong?" Paul said.

"Could you please come down to the library, Mr. Miller. I want to show you something."

"Why can't you just tell me what it is?" Paul said.

"It's hard to explain," Lynn said. "I think you should see for yourself."

"All right," Paul said. "I'll be right down."

"What is it?" Susan asked when Paul had closed the door.

"I don't know," Paul said. "Something in the library that Lynn is upset about. I'll go and take a look and be right back."

When Paul returned a few minutes later, his face was set in grim lines.

"What's wrong?" Susan asked.

"Our mysterious poet has struck again!" Paul said.

While Susan dressed, Paul went to wake the others. They all met downstairs in the library. The first thing they saw was the axe, its blade sunk into the back of a chair. There was a note lying next to it. Jerry read it aloud.

"The judge and jury did agree,
That Lizzie Borden should go free.
Stealing is an ugly crime,
The thief should pay and now's the time!"

"Before anybody starts blaming us," Paul said, "I just want you to know that Susan and I didn't have anything to do with this!"

"Nobody said you did," said Basil. "Where's the hired help?"

"Lynn's in the kichen," Paul said. "I don't know where Bert is. I'll say this for Lynn. She was really upset when she came to tell me about finding this. I don't think it was an act."

"How can you be sure?" Susan asked. "We don't know anything about her."

"Wait a minute," Stephanie said. "*Now* I remember where I've seen Lynn before. It was just before our last weekend. She came over to me in a coffee shop at lunchtime one day. She said she had found out that I worked for you, Uncle Basil. She wanted me to give you a short story she'd written. I told her I couldn't do that. I told her to post it to the editor. Mona, do you remember ever getting a story from Lynn Cutler?"

Mona shook her head. "I can't remember all the stories I get in the post. There are too many."

"Was this story supposed to be for *Mysteries for Midnight Reading?"* Basil asked.

Stephanie nodded. "But I guess her story didn't get published. Unless —" She stared at the group, her eyes wide. "Do you suppose that she is J. R. Thompson?"

"I doubt it," Basil said. "I can't believe that a beginning writer would write under a different name. And then go out of her way to keep her real identity a secret. The publicity would be too important."

"That's true," Susan said. "What about Bert? Maybe he was upset because Lynn's story wasn't used. Maybe this is his way of getting even."

"You have a good point there," Jerry said. "I think it's time we talked to young Bert."

"Aren't we forgetting something?" Mona said. "This is the second time the mysterious poet has written about a thief. Now what do you suppose was stolen?"

Everyone shrugged.

"Maybe Bert and Lynn can tell us," Jerry said. "I say it's time we stopped playing guessing games. We have to find out who left the notes. Once we know, maybe we'll learn the answers to all our questions. For now, Bert and Lynn are our best suspects."

"I agree," said Teri. "They had the best opportunity to plant both those notes. Go and get them, Paul."

A few minutes later Paul returned to the library with Bert and Lynn. Lynn looked frightened, but Bert was angry.

"I understand you think we wrote those notes," he said before anyone else could say a word.

"We think it's very possible," Susan said.

Bert gave her an ugly smile. "I thought you people were so good at mysteries," he said. "You call yourselves the Masters of Mystery! Ha! I bet you can't even find a pair of lost socks!"

"So you *are* guilty," Teri said.

"No," Bert said. "We didn't write those notes. Why should we? If you want to play stupid little games, what does it matter to us?"

"It's not a game," Stephanie said. "I think one of you had a reason to write those notes. You, Lynn! You tried to pass a story to Mr. Hunter through me, but I wouldn't take it. Maybe you and your friend Bert decided to get even with me."

Lynn stared at Stephanie with her mouth open. "That's not fair!"

"Did you send the story to the editor as I told you to?" Stephanie said.

"Yes, I did," Lynn said. "And it was returned to me. But that's not the first time I've had a story turned down. It's no big deal. It happens to all writers."

"What about you, Bert?" Teri said. "You might have wanted to get even with Basil Hunter because Lynn's story was turned down."

"Yes, and both of you had the opportunity to plant both the notes," Paul said.

"Maybe we had the opportunity," Bert said. "But we didn't do it! And you can't prove that we did."

"He has a point," Basil said. "We can't prove that they did. Maybe they had a reason, and maybe they had an opportunity. But that doesn't mean they did it. And we can't figure out this business about something being stolen."

"Now you're saying we stole something?" Bert cried. "Boy, that does it! I'm not going to stay here for the rest of the weekend with a bunch of crazy people."

"Bert, no! We need the money," Lynn said.

"Not that bad," Bert said. "Come on, let's go and pack our bags. The sooner we're out of here, the better."

He took Lynn by the arm and pulled her out of the room. Susan sank onto the couch. "I don't believe it!" she said.

"Well, I'm glad it's over," Paul said. "Now we can get our weekend back on track. How about getting us some coffee, Susan?"

"Okay," Susan said. "I could do with a cup of coffee right now."

"I'll come with you," Mona said. "We can get breakfast and then get on with the fun."

Stephanie offered to set the table. The three women left the room. Jerry pulled the axe out of the back of the chair. "This was an ugly thing to have happened," Jerry said. "But I hope no one will let it spoil the rest of the weekend."

"I'm just glad we got rid of those two." Basil said. "I wish we could have proved which one of them left the notes. I'm going to phone that agency on Monday morning and report Bert."

At that moment they heard the front door open and close. Paul went to the window. "There they go," he said.

"Good!" said Basil, rubbing his hands. "Jerry, throw some wood on the fire, will you? It's cold in here."

"Well, Paul," Teri said, "what's the plan for the rest of the day? Are we —"

Suddenly they heard the front door bang open. A moment later Bert stood in the doorway of the library. He was very angry.

"Forget something?" Jerry asked.

"Listen, this has gone too far," Bert snapped. "Which one of you messed with my car?"

"What are you talking about?" Paul asked.

"I can't start my car," Bert said. "The distributor cap is missing. Now stop fooling around, and give it back!"

CHAPTER

6

Searching the House

Susan came hurrying from the kitchen with Stephanie right behind her. "What's going on?" they asked.

"Something is wrong with Bert's car," Paul said. "I'll go and take a look." He began to put on his coat.

"We'll all come with you," Jerry said. He reached for his coat, too.

Everyone crowded outside onto the wide front porch, looking at the yard. The rain had stopped sometime in the night, but the yard was a sea of mud and wet leaves. "Be careful, everyone," Jerry said. "It's going to be messy out here."

"What's going on?" Mona said, joining them on the porch. Susan told her, and Mona went to get her coat.

Bert's car had seen better days. It was covered with dents and rust. They stood in a group around it while Paul and Jerry looked under the bonnet. "Well, he's right," Paul said. "The distributor cap is missing."

"What about the other cars?" Basil asked. They all looked at each other and then went to check. It was soon clear that none of the cars worked.

"This is very strange," Jerry said. "All the distributor caps are missing. Why would Bert steal his own? In fact, why would he do anything to the cars at all?"

"So you don't think he's the one who wrote those notes?" Teri said.

Jerry shrugged. "I have to believe that the notes and the stolen distributor caps were done by the same person. It makes no sense for Bert to have messed up his own car."

"We are the Masters of Mystery," Paul said. "We have always been proud of the way we could solve a mystery. Now we have a real one on our hands. We aren't going about this the right way."

"I agree," Mona said. "I think we should all go back to the house and talk this whole thing over."

"It wouldn't hurt to call a mechanic," Basil said. "Does this place have a phone, Paul?"

"In the library," Paul said.

They started back to the house. Suddenly with a cry, Mona slipped and fell. Jerry ran to his wife. "Are you all right?" he asked.

"I hurt my ankle," she said.

Susan checked Mona's ankle. "Nothing seems to be broken," she said. "I think it's just sprained."

Jerry carried Mona to the library and put her on the couch. Paul went upstairs to get the first-aid kit. Basil picked up the phone. He listened for a moment and then frowned. He held up the phone wire. It had been cut. "Someone wants to make sure we don't go anywhere," he said.

They all stared at each other in silence. Lynn turned to Bert, her eyes wide with fear. "I don't like this," she whispered. "Can't we just walk out of here?"

"It's too far to try to make it on foot," Susan said. "You would never get through those woods. They're too thick. And it's miles down that road. It may start to rain again at any time. I really think you should stay here."

"Knowing how you feel about us?" Bert said.

"I think we made a mistake," Jerry said. "Please accept our apologies. Right now I'd have to say we're all suspects."

At that moment Paul came back with the first-aid kit. Susan began to clean Mona's leg. "You have some bad cuts and scratches," she said, seeing the pain on Mona's face.

As Susan was bandaging Mona's cuts, Stephanie said, "I've been thinking, Susan, you said this is a big house. Is it possible that someone else could be hiding here?"

"Boy, that's a good question," Jerry said. "Paul, you said you and Susan only cleaned the rooms we would use this weekend. Have you been all over the house?"

Paul shook his head. "We looked at a few of the rooms on the third floor. But we didn't go into the attic or down to the cellar. And there's a barn and some sheds outside. I think what Stepanie said makes sense."

"I think we should search the place," Basil said. "Just to be on the safe side."

"I agree," Jerry said. "Okay, Mona, I'll take you upstairs to our room now."

"No way," Mona said. "I don't want to be left all alone up there."

"But upstairs you can lock the door. You can't lock the library door," Jerry said.

"I don't care," Mona said. "It's nice and warm down here. Besides, I'm not afraid. No one has been hurt, Jerry."

"Mona has a good point," Basil said. "So far we've just been scared and upset, but not hurt. Okay, everyone, why don't we break into teams. Stephanie and I will take the attic."

Paul and Susan agreed to search the third floor. And Teri and Jerry said they would search the cellar. "I just hope there aren't any rats down there," Teri said. "I hate rats!"

"What about us?" Bert said.

"You and Lynn can check the barn and the sheds," Paul said. "Maybe you'll find those missing distributor caps too."

Bert nodded. The teams went in different directions, leaving Mona in the library. "Don't worry about me," she said cheerfully. "If I get scared, I'll scream my head off."

Twenty minutes later, they all met back at the library. "No luck," Basil said, wiping dust from his hands. "The attic is full of interesting stuff. But I don't think anyone has been up there for years. The dust on the floor is thick and we saw no footprints."

"That's also true for the rooms on the third floor," Paul said.

"We found nothing in the cellar," Jerry said.

"That's not exactly true," Teri said. "We did find rats!" She shivered.

Paul grinned. "How about you, Bert?"

Bert shook his head. "No sign that anyone has been in the barn or the sheds," he said. "And no distributor caps, either."

"We don't seem to be getting anywhere," Susan said.

"What about that coffee?" Jerry asked. "I could really do with a cup. And something to eat, too. I don't think well on an empty stomach."

"Oh, goodness," Susan said. "The coffee will be cold by now. I shall make a fresh pot and get busy with the food."

Lynn and Bert offered to help. "It beats sitting around, doing nothing," Lynn said. "And, after all, that's what we were hired to do."

Jerry threw more wood on the fire. "I do wish I knew where those distributor caps were," he said. "All of us have to get out of here tomorrow and we —"

He was cut off by a sharp cry from the kitchen. It was Susan and she sounded very upset.

CHAPTER

7

Suspects All

Everyone ran to the kitchen to see what was wrong. They found Susan, Lynn, and Bert staring at a new note. It was leaning against the coffee pot. The cups on the table were filled with coffee that had long ago turned cold. but there was something else as well — a strong smell of almonds was in the air.

Susan picked up the note and read it aloud. Her voice shook as she said:

"Poison is a woman's tool,
But one who steals is also cruel.
The clue is in the newest book.
To catch a thief, that's where you'll look!"

"Last night we talked about poison," Stephanie said. "Just the way we talked about Lizzie Borden and Jack the Ripper. We've had notes about those two killers and now we have this one about poison. Jerry, do you think there is poison in the coffee?"

"Susan, do you have the almond flavouring you put in the pudding?" Jerry asked.

She nodded and handed him the bottle. "It was a new bottle," she said. "I used very little. But the bottle is almost empty."

"I think our poet wanted to scare us," Jerry said. "I doubt that there is poison in the coffee. But none of us wants to drink that cold mess anyway. Pour it away, Susan, and we'll start again."

"What about the food?" Teri said.

"I'm not taking any chances," Lynn said. "I'm going to cook a new meal."

"I think we should all stay together in the kitchen while we get breakfast," Susan said. No one said a word, but everyone knew what she was thinking. None of them could trust anyone else. "I'll get Mona," Jerry said.

When the meal was ready, everyone sat down at the kitchen table to eat. After they had finished, Jerry said, "That was very good, Lynn. Thank you. I feel a lot better."

"I have an idea," Basil said. "We've been running around in circles all morning. It's time we got serious about solving this mystery."

"Where do we start?" Teri said.

"The notes go along with the theme of the weekend," Basil said. "Let's start there,"

"Now hold on," Paul said. "Susan and I kept the theme a secret until after dinner. From then on we were all together in the library. So how could our poet have planted that first note in time for Stephanie to find it?"

"Wait, Paul," Susan said. "Remember when you and I were in the kichen last night before dinner? We were talking about the weekend then. I thought I heard someone in the dining room."

"That's right," Paul said. "I forgot about that."

"I think someone overheard us talking and came up with the idea before dinner."

"Poison pen letters," Teri said suddenly.

"What?" Stephanie looked puzzled.

"Poison pen letters are written to hurt people," Teri said. "The writer doesn't sign his or her name. They are supposed to scare the person who reads them."

"How do you know so much about poison pen letters?" Mona asked.

"I've used them in a couple of the mysteries I've written," Teri said. "You don't think *I* wrote those poems, do you?"

"Hold on," Jerry said. "Let's not start blaming each other. We won't get anywhere if we start doing that. We have to figure this thing out step by step. Okay, first of all, we know that one of us must be the poet. And we know that he or she overheard Susan and Paul talking about the theme in the kitchen before dinner."

"That would have given the person enough time to write the first note and put it in the bathroom," Paul said. "And also to steal the knife from the box in the library," he added.

"Stephanie, you were last to come down before dinner," Jerry said.

"But I didn't leave that note!" Stephanie cried. "You have to believe me!"

"But we were all together from then on," Basil said.

"No, we weren't" said Susan. "Teri, you went up to change your clothes after you spilled soup on them."

"Now wait a minute —" Teri said.

"All we're trying to do is to place everyone," Jerry said. "Did anyone else go upstairs after Teri did?"

"Yes," said Susan. "Stephanie and Mona went up after dinner."

"Were the two of you together the whole time?" Jerry asked.

Stephanie shook her head. Then she said, "Bert and Lynn had the opportunity, too. And they weren't with us in the library."

"Now hold on," Bert said sharply. "I thought we weren't suspects."

"What we are saying," Jerry said, "Is that five of us had an easy opportunity to plant the first note. Any of us could have planted the second one and stolen those distributor caps. That could have been done during the night. What about the third note?"

"Mona and Stephanie and I were in the kitchen getting breakfast," Susan said. "There was no note then. We all went outside to check the cars. When we came back, Paul left the library to get the first-aid kit."

"But we would have seen Paul if he'd gone into the kitchen," Teri said. "The library door was wide open."

"And there's no other way to get to the kitchen," Susan said.

"We broke into teams after that," Jerry said. "We went to search the house and buildings outside."

"Mona was alone in the library during that time," Stephanie said.

"Yes, but she had a sprained ankle," said Susan. "I don't think she would have been able to walk on it so quickly to get to the kitchen and back."

"But you would have seen anyone else who went into the kitchen," Stephanie said.

"I saw no one," Mona said.

"This is stupid," Bert said. "You people aren't getting anywhere. A fine group of detectives you turned out to be!"

"Slow down, Bert," Jerry said. "These things take time. At least we all know where everyone was when the three notes were planted. Now, what about those poems? What do they mean?"

"Well, one of us is good at coming up with clever poems on the spur of the moment," Susan said.

"Oh, right!" Bert laughed. "A real Shakespeare!"

"The poems mention the criminals we talked about last night. Criminals who were never caught or who were set free," said Basil. "And each note mentions a thief and something that was stolen. Could that be a crime that was never solved?"

"The last note mentions a clue being in the newest book," said Paul. "Last night we talked about your new book, Basil."

"And" said Jerry, "We talked about the mysterious writer, J. R. Thompson." He looked at each of them with a small smile. "What if J. R. Thompson is one of us?"

CHAPTER

8

One Mystery Solved

"J. R. Thompson, one of us?" Susan said. "Really, Jerry, that's crazy!"

"Maybe not," Jerry said. "Remember I told you I spent some time watching the post office. No one came to get J. R. Thompson's mail. Maybe that was because the writer saw me and knew who I was. Someone in this group.

"But if one of us is J. R. Thompson, why hide the fact?" Stephanie asked.

"I thought about that," Jerry said. "And the only answer that makes any sense is that the story itself was stolen."

Paul shook his head. "I don't understand, Jerry. You're saying that one of us stole a story and sent it to Basil under the name J. R. Thompson? Even if that were true, what do the notes have to do with that?"

"Well," Jerry said slowly, "This is the part I don't like. Suppose the real author of the story is also one of us. Now, Paul, if you had written that story, how would you feel knowing one of your best friends ripped it off."

Paul took a deep breath and let it out slowly. "I see what you mean, Jerry. It would nearly kill me to think that a good friend would do something that low."

Jerry nodded. "It's a pretty ugly idea," he said. "But I think it makes sense. And it clears up the business of those notes. I think our poet is the real author of the story. And he or she is trying to 'smoke out' the person who stole the story."

"I don't know," Basil said. "It's a little thin, Jerry. Do you have any other proof?"

"Well, let's think about last weekend together. You were worried about finding another story, Basil. Then a couple of weeks later, you got a story in the post, I think the story was stolen when we were all together. If the writer and the thief are members of our group, then that weekend was the time the story could have been stolen. This weekend would be the first real chance the writer had to find out who stole it."

"So why is the writer leaving those stupid

notes?" Bert asked.

They all turned to stare at him. It was the first time he had shown any interest in the mystery.

"I think maybe the writer hopes to find out who the thief is without giving himself or herself away," Jerry said.

"Well, I don't like it," Susan said. "I wish the writer had told Paul and me what was going on. After all, the weekend is pretty well ruined as far as I'm concerned."

"I understand how upset you are," Jerry said. "You and Paul went to a lot of trouble to make this weekend a success, Susan. But what if *you're* the thief!"

Susan stared at Jerry with her mouth open. "How can you say that?" she said.

"Jerry is right," Basil said. "It could be any of us. But someone is doing a good job of hiding their movements to confuse the rest of us."

"We've been through all of this already," Paul said. "There was no one in the kitchen when Susan, Mona and Stephanie went to get breakfast. Then we were all together outside while we checked the cars. Later we were all together in the library. There was no chance for someone to plant that third note without being seen!"

"Unless," Susan said. She stopped, and frowned.

"Unless what?" Teri said.

Susan was silent for a moment longer. Then she said, "Of couse! Why didn't I see it before! There is only one person who could have left that last note and the first two as well!"

"Who? Paul asked.

His wife looked at each of them, her eyes filled with sadness. "Now I see why our poet hated to say anything. It's awful to look into the face of a friend and wonder if that is the one. But I guess I'll have to say what I think, anyway. I think our mysterious poet is Mona."

They all looked from Susan to Mona. She didn't say a word. But Jerry leaned forward, his eyes filled with anger.

"How can you say that, Susan? You and Mona have been good friends for years."

"Wait a minute, Jerry," Paul said quietly. "Look, no matter who Susan named, someone would be upset. I think we should hear her out. She must have some reason for saying what she did."

Jerry took a deep breath and leaned back in his chair. "You're right. Paul. Okay, Susan.

Why don't you tell us why you think Mona is the poet."

"We agreed that five of us could have planted the first note," Susan said. "Any of us could have planted the second one and only four of us could have planted the last one. Mona and Stephanie were in all three groups.

"No," Jerry said. "This morning Mona sprained her ankle."

"I think the note was put in the kitchen before we all went outside," Susan said. "We were all on the porch together. The last person to join us was Mona. She had just enough time to put the almond flavouring in the coffee and to leave the note."

"That's not much proof," Basil said.

"There's more," Susan said. "Last night Mona went upstairs to get her knitting. She had more than enough time to plant the note while she was upstairs."

"It's still thin evidence," Jerry said.

"Finally there's this," Susan said. "When I was looking at Mona's ankle, I saw a lot of bad cuts and scratches. They weren't the kind of scrapes you get from falling in the mud. But they *were* the kind of scratches you'd get from going into the woods to hide those distributor caps.

There was a moment of silence and everyone turned to look at Mona. Her face had gone quite pale. Jerry reached out to take his wife's hand. "Honey, it isn't true, is it?"

Mona took a deep breath. She looked at her husband and at each member of the group. Then she nodded. "Yes, it's true. I'm the one that left the notes, and I stole the distributor caps."

Jerry groaned. "Mona, why didn't you come to me in the beginning and tell me?"

"I couldn't," Mona said. "I don't know why, but I just couldn't bring myself to talk about it. You see, I'd been working on that story for months. I've always wanted to be a writer. Oh, don't get me wrong. I love my job as an editor. But after editing other writer's stories for years, I wanted to see if I could turn out my own original story."

She took a deep breath while the others waited. Then she went on. "It all happened pretty much the way Susan said it did. After our last weekend together, Basil got the story in the post. I remember that day so well. He came into my office and he was so happy and excited. He said he'd found the last story for his book. He said it was one of the best short stories he'd ever read. Then he gave it to me to read."

"It must have been a terrible shock to see your story under someone else's name," Paul said.

Mona nodded. "I read the first few lines and at first I was just puzzled. But then as I went on reading. I knew this was no accident. It was *my* story. The names of the characters had been changed, but that's about all. It was my plot all the way through. At first I couldn't understand how this had happened. But then it hit me. Someone had read my story and stolen it. I was so angry I felt sick."

"Why didn't you say something?" Basil asked.

I guess I didn't know if you would believe me," Mona said. "I went a little crazy for a while. Then I tried to work out who could have stolen the story, and how they could have done it. At first I thought it might have been someone at work. But then I remembered that once I had half the story written, I had stopped taking it to the office. I only worked on it at home."

"But you have other friends," Stephanie said. "Couldn't it have been one of them?"

"I thought about that, too," Mona said. "But you see, I kept it in the bottom drawer of my desk. None of my other friends ever had a reason to go into my desk. And then I remembered our weekend together!"

"What about it?" Paul asked. "What made you suspect one of us?"

"That was the last time we were together. All of us gathered at our house that weekend. When I thought back, I remembered that several of you had needed to get something from my desk or wanted to use the telephone in that room."

Mona paused for a moment. The others in the room looked at one another with suspicion.

Mona went on. "We've all been friends for such a long time that at first I couldn't believe it. But the more I thought about it, the more I decided that that was the only time the story could have been stolen."

"I had no idea," Jerry said slowly, shaking his head. "No idea at all. You hid your feelings very well, Mona."

"When I finally decided it was one of you, I wanted to find the thief and somehow get even," Mona said. "I wanted this so-called friend to feel the same pain I felt. As time went on, I tried to come up with a plan. I thought about sending you all letters — the kind Teri would call 'poison pen' letters. But I wasn't sure that would work. Besides, I wanted to see the thief's face. I kept coming up with one plan after another. Nothing seemed to be just what I wanted."

"When did you come up with the idea for leaving the poems," Susan said.

"Just as you suspected, Susan. When I was in the dining room, I overheard you and Paul talking in the kitchen. You see, when I got here Friday night, I became upset almost at once."

"I wondered if you felt well," Susan said. "I remember how quiet and pale you were when you got here."

"It was almost more than I could stand to be in the same room with all of you," Mona said. "To have to talk and smile and act as if nothing were wrong. I tried to rest for a while before dinner, but my head began to ache. I decided to come downstairs to see if you had anything I could take for it, Susan. When I got to the dining room, I overheard you and Paul. That's when I got the idea for the notes. The theme for the weekend was perfect for what I wanted to do. Unsolved crimes! Yes, it was just perfect!"

She smiled but the smile never reached her eyes.

"What I didn't think of," Mona said, "Was that all of you are good at solving mysteries. I don't know why I thought I could make the thief come forward and confess. I should have realised this plan was stupid."

They were all silent for a few moments. Then Stephanie said, "We have to find out who the thief is. If we don't, more than this one weekend will be ruined. After all, Mona will never be able to trust any of us again. She will always wonder who stole her story."

'We'll all wonder," Paul said.

"If only the thief will come out and confess," Jerry said.

There was a long, cold silence. Then Susan said. "It isn't going to work, Jerry. The person who stole that story will never confess."

They all fell quiet again. Mona began to cry very softly. The others stared at the floor silently.

"You aren't going to give up, are you?" The voice made them jump a little. It was Bert. He leaned forward in his chair, staring at them. "Look here, you can't just give up now!"

Basil groaned. "Come on, Bert. Think about what you're saying. You're asking us to solve a crime that happened a year ago. We have no clues!"

"How do you know?" Bert asked. "You aren't even going to try! Look, I know I made fun of you. I laughed at this whole group and the idea behind it. But now I'm having second thoughts. I listened to the way you put the clues together to solve the business of those notes. And I have to admit that you people are sharp. If you solved the first mystery, why can't you solve the second one?"

"He's right," Lynn said. "You've got to try. You have to find out which person is the thief!"

Paul nodded. "I think we have to try."

Stephanie looked excited. "Yes, why not? We don't have anything else to do. Besides, that's why we came here this weekend. To solve a mystery."

"Unsolved crimes," Susan laughed. "Little did Paul and I know when we picked that theme that we would have a real unsolved crime on our hands."

CHAPTER

9

A Thief Uncovered

"We have to go back to that weekend we were together," Jerry said.

"You said the story was in your desk, Mona," Paul said. "I suppose you hadn't locked the drawer.

"I had no reason to," Mona said. "I trusted everyone."

"Some of us used your desk that weekend," Stephanie said.

"You all had one reason or another to use my desk or enter the study," Mona said. "I spent a lot of time thinking about it in the weeks that followed," she added.

"What do you remember, Mona?" Jerry asked.

"Well, Susan was looking for some scissors to cut out some book reviews from the newspaper. I told her she could find a pair in my desk. And Paul asked to use the telephone in the study to call a book dealer.

"I think I do remember calling someone that weekend," Paul said.

"Anyone else?" Jerry asked.

"I'm not sure Basil ever went in there," Mona said. "But I know Stephanie did. She asked to use my typewriter. Something about typing business letters for you, Basil."

"That's right. I remember now." Stephanie said. "I was a little angry at Uncle Basil for making me work on a weekend."

"Speaking of work," Susan said, "you were still working on your book, weren't you Teri?"

"Oh, just notes for some changes I wanted to make," Teri said. "I wouldn't say I really worked on the book."

"But you did need some paper," Mona said. "I remember you asked me for some the moment you got to my house on Friday."

Teri laughed. "So I did. I'd been thinking about some changes I wanted to make while I was driving to your house. I wanted to make some notes because I was afraid I'd forget them by Monday."

"So most of us did have a reason to be near

Mona's desk at some time during the weekend," Paul said. "That means any of us could have seen the story and stolen it."

"Maybe not," Mona said. "I mean, it was a long story and it had a lot of twists and turns to it. I don't think anyone would have been able to remember the plot without a copy of the story."

"Which means one of us had to get it copied," Basil said. "It would have taken too long to type it out. The person who stole it had to get it out of the house to get a copy made."

"But we were all together," Stephanie said.

"Not quite," Susan said, her eyes flashing. "Paul, we were talking about that yesterday, remember? One of us left for a while on Saturday afternoon."

"Teri!" Paul said. "You went out to buy some steaks."

"That's because I burnt the first lot." Teri said. "Don't you remember? But that doesn't make me a thief!"

"I wondered why you offered to help cook dinner that night," Susan said. "We all know you hate to cook. But you said you would cook the steaks, I think you found Mona's story on

Friday night. You read it and thought it was good. And you saw a way to make some money from it. But you had to have a copy of it. So that's why you offered to cook the steaks. You burnt them on purpose. Then you took the story with you when you went to buy more meat. And that's when you made the copy!"

"Oh, *really!*" Teri said. "Why would I steal Mona's story? I'm a pretty good writer myself, you know."

"For the money," Susan said. "You knew Basil needed another story for his book. But you were still working on your own book. You didn't have time to write a new story for him. But you needed the money!"

"That's ridiculous," Teri cried.

"Is it?" Susan said. "Last night you told us you still hadn't finished that book. It's been more than two years since you published a book. But you buy a new car every year and you wear beautiful clothes and jewels. Where do you get the money to live like that?"

"Is that all your evidence?" Teri said, her eyes narrowed with anger.

"No," Susan said. "Last night you said you never wrote short stories. But you used to. In the newest mystery magazine there is a copy of a short story you wrote years ago. I think you wanted to have something in Basil's new book, but you didn't have time.

"Then you came across Mona's story by accident. You had the story copied, you changed the names of the characters and a few other things here and there. Then you sent it to Basil under a different name. And you did everything you could to keep him from finding out who J. R. Thompson really was."

Teri said nothing. Her face had gone quite pale.

"Teri!" Basil said sharply. "Is it true? Did *you* steal that story from Mona?"

Teri looked at Basil. "I had too," she said coldly. "I had a lot of bills to pay. And I couldn't seem to finish the book I was writing. I still can't seem to finish it."

"So you've got a case of writer's block," Mona said. "All writers get that. That's no reason to steal someone else's story," she added angrily.

Teri shrugged and stood up. I'm going upstairs to pack. I guess you won't want to see me again. Well, that's fine with me."

"Wait a minute," Paul said sharply. "Aren't you even going to say you're sorry, Teri?

"Sorry? The only thing I'm sorry about is that I got caught."

Her friends watched her go in silence. They were too shocked to speak. It was Basil who broke the silence.

"Boy, what a weekend!" he said. "Mona, I'm sorry about all of this."

"It's not your fault, Basil," she said.

"I shouldn't have published that story until I had learned for certain who J. R. Thompson was." He paused and then said, "But I'm going to make things right. You know we're going to print 50,000 more copies of *Mysteries for Midnight Reading* next month. Well, in the new edition, the name on that story will be *Mona Rice.*"

Mona gave Basil a big smile. "Thank you," she said.

"What about our group?" Susan asked. "What's going to happen to the Masters of Mystery?"

"Teri is gone — and I say good riddance," Jerry said. "But we can't let this ruin what we have. Our friendship, these weekends together, our love of mysteries. And don't forget, there are still some crimes we haven't solved."

"Such as?" Basil said.

"Such as Lizzie Borden's crime. Did she murder her stepmother and her father? Now I think —"

Paul and Susan smiled at each other. Maybe the weekend could be saved after all.